VERY CLOSE AND VERY SLOW

The Wesleyan Poetry Program: Volume 76

Very Close and Very Slow

by
JUDITH HEMSCHEMEYER

Wesleyan University Press

MIDDLETOWN, CONNECTICUT

Acknowledgement is gratefully made to *Cimmaron* and to *The Western Humanities Review*, in the pages of which two of the poems in this book were first published.

The publisher gratefully acknowledges the support of the publication of this book by The Andrew W. Mellon Foundation.

Library of Congress Cataloging in Publication Data

Hemschemeyer, Judith.
    Very close and very slow.

    (The Wesleyan poetry program, v. 76)
    Poems.
    I. Title.
PS3558.E4795V4   811'.5'4   74–20951
ISBN 0–8195–2076–4
ISBN 0–8195–1076–9 (pbk.)

Manufactured in the United States of America
First edition

Contents

I

Vocation

The day I finally decided
To be a poet—yesterday—
I found I had everything I needed:

A clean pair of jeans,
Half a bottle of bourbon

My four-inch brass policeman paperweight

My sandstone Cochiti mountain lion fetish
With its soul strapped to its side

And an owl's cough-ball,
A bundle of matchstick mousebones
Floating in a puff of fur.

The Sisters

An Irishwoman in a German town,
my grandma spent her days alone,
longing for her sister Nellie's visits
from Freeport, Illinois.

Then, my father said, they made a day of it:

They heated pots of water,
stacked dry towels on the sink,
told the kids to run outside,
stripped off their shirtwaists,
fished out all the pins
and washed and rinsed each other's long black hair
and dried it on the back porch in the sun.

And oh, the feast of talk there must have been,
the biscuits and the fragrant cups of tea.

How idle and soft and fine their hands
lay in their laps for once and how keen
the scent of the vinegar
they had added to the last rinse
so their manes of hair would shine.

The Idiot

'Schüttel dich, Fritz!'
'Shake yourself!'

my mother said
the kids would tell him
on their way to school.

And at dusk
when they repassed the asylum
he would still be clinging to the bars

still shaking
but more slowly

or flopped exhausted in the weeds
waiting for them
to tell him to stop.

We Interrupt This Broadcast

They're still my grown-ups
and it's still Sunday afternoon
beneath the table.

It's raining blackjack
but my oak protects me
from the Plock! 'Hit me!' Plock!

Motionless, I scurry
in and out of their talk,
hauling back huge wisdoms.

A miscarriage is messy
and I think it has
high, wobbly wheels.

Time and a half
needs a fatter clock.
'Hit me!' Plock! 'Too hard!' Laugh.

War is coming but not yet.
There's still half a jug
of sour honey-colored beer

and mother just lit a cigarette.
Hitler could kill me
but he'd have to fight

Roosevelt, Joe Louis
and Daddy to get into the house.
Anyway, I'm a mouse.

12

At Our House

— to Meg

Because everything
we did on paper
got crumpled up
and thrown away

or,
if it was a secret,
read,

we stopped trusting paper.

You drew your skinny angels
on the rough, dark boards
of the garage

and I wrote,
as far back on the furnace pipe
as I could reach

March 10, 1948. Grandpa is dead.

The Old Priest

Subbing for our sick one
he took us by surprise

wandering slow-motion
through the Mass like that.

At the Confiteor
he really confessed;

his face — from the side at least —
was stiff with guilt.

By then the altar boys
had his number

and they smirked to let us know
they were keeping their heads.

But they too sat helpless
during his sun-drenched sermon

watching his lips twitch, his eyes close
and his hands move through the motes.

What was he whispering
I remember wondering

and to whom?

Walking Home from Gone With the Wind

Walking home from *Gone With the Wind*
I got so worked up

I made my cousin stop
by the woods to talk about it.

Burning like Atlanta
with the thirst for fierce adventures

I made her tell me what she was going to be
when she grew up. She shrugged.

'I just want to get married,' she said,
'and have a bunch of kids.'

And I remember the surge of pity
I felt for her, for the dull life she had picked.

But she was stubborn;
she grew up and married a handsome sailor

and moved down to Alabama
and had four kids

and raised them mostly by herself,
he being at sea

and had a nervous breakdown
and came back from it

and this spring lost her oldest daughter
in a flaming crash on prom night. . . .

I remember shaking my fist like Scarlet
but I forget what I vowed I was going to be.

Now for a Few Days

Now for a few days
Translucent tulips
Float across the lawns

Branches in blossom
Press against the house
Until it hums

The green-gold hours slide
Away, smooth as eels
Behind glass walls. And now

For someone, somewhere
Kneeling to plant, comes
The grace note, the first stroke.

My Mother's Death

It's still inside me

like that ninety-pound fibroid tumor
in that woman's womb.

Unable to lie down or walk,
she could only kneel.

It took two doctors to lift it out of her,
the paper said.

But who will help me.

To My Sister in Her Grief

Either quote *Thanatopsis*
—'her favorite poem'—

or don't quote it.

But don't stand here
beside her body
saying over and over
to whoever will listen

'So live,
that when thy something something comes . . .'

and turning to me for the words.

The Survivors

Night after night
She dreamed we were drowned
Or covered with spiders
Or butchered or tortured

She took us all to bed with her

And woke up whimpering
And came to find our bodies
In the dark, brushing our foreheads
Sorting out our tangled limbs

Amazed to find us whole

By day her love for us
Was a prairie fire
That roared across our whole horizon
Burning us out of our burrows

'I touched the windowpane'
'I touched myself'
'I let the boys touch me'

Like small, crazed animals
We leaped before her
Knowing there was no escape

She had to consume us utterly
Over and over again

And now at last
We are her angels
Burned so crisp
We crumble when we try to touch

The Dirty-billed Freeze Footy

Remember that Saturday morning
Mother forgot the word gull?

We were all awake but still in bed
and she called out, 'Hey kids!

What's the name of that bird that eats garbage
and stands around in cold water on the beach?'

And you, the quick one, the youngest daughter
piped right back: 'A dirty-billed freeze footy!'

And she laughed till she was weak,
until it hurt her. And you had done it:

reduced our queen to warm and helpless rubble.

And the rest of the day, baking or cleaning
or washing our hair until it squeaked,

whenever she caught sight of you
it would start all over again.

Very Close and Very Slow

As usual
I panned the faces
very close and very slow.

Yours
was almost as big as Spain
and just as beautiful,
with its dramatic ridges,
perfect mouth.

But you complained about your eyes.
You couldn't see, you said.

So I zoomed in on them:
one was milky,
the other solid silver

and suddenly it was up to me
to tell you that it didn't matter

to tell you,
as gently as I could,
that you were dead.

II

Oak Staircase

In my dream it staggers up and up,
creaking round its corners like a tired purse snatcher,
canting like a drunk

from a base so far below
I've lost sight of it.

Naturally, no walls have been issued
so it's only a matter of time. . . .

I'm always last in line,
there's lots of light
and I don't know why we're inching upward

only that the whole structure,
a cobra hypnotized against its will,
is swaying, waiting for the moment to collapse.

The worst is when the others,
who have been there,
shoulder past us on their slow way down

silent, but so dedicated to survival
they peel off our handholds
when we get in their way.

If it weren't for the finish:
shellac and wax rubbed to a mellow glow

and the grain: paramecia twitching apart
on the landing post

and on the rail beneath my hand
a contour map of mountains . . . no!

Oh God! the peaks themselves
leaping at me as I wake and drop!

Philoxenos

In Greece we were never alone.

When we took walks we would meet women
standing in the path spinning yarn

waiting to invite us in for water
and that sticky, sugared fruit *gleeká*.

They patted my belly
and prophesied my son.

They watched over us,
passing us from island to island,
from hand to hand.

Giving Birth in Greek

Giving birth in Greek
only took two words.

The midwife smoothed my hair,
coaxed my legs into stirrups
and gave me the shot

that sent my head
high into a corner
of that dazzling room

from where I watched it all.

There was a wild animal
stuck inside me,
struggling to get out

and I could see
I was doing everything I could
to help it:

breathing evenly,
exhaling at the crest
of the contractions

not pushing

still not pushing

giving those muscles,
those raw, stubborn snails,
one last chance to break my back

and mold me into whatever shape
it needed to escape.

Then all at once
it was that moment
when I knew if I pushed
I would die

and if I didn't push
I would die
but it would still be inside me

and '*Tora!*' 'Now!' she shouted

and we both bore down
and the beast became my son
and slid into her hands.

'*Oraia*,' 'Beautiful,'
she said. '*Oraia.*'

Later, in my room, in the dark,
I started to bleed a lot
and I knew I should call the nurse

but I didn't know the words.

Anyway there were no more words.

I lay all night
in that cold, clotting stain,
wide open, wide awake

and falling in love
all over again.

31

This Morning

Soft green of a postage stamp from Poland
Soft blue of the sky

The chairs are half wood
Half light

The plants want to be watered
Then left alone

Some days I'm a minor priestess on probation
In my own house

I'm allowed to shift things
But only slightly

Slice a lemon, pack brown sugar
In a blue-green Mason jar

Certain Themes Emerge

After a number of years
Certain themes emerge,
From the back pages of the paper:

Tourists are jamming
The slopes of Mount Etna today.
Hoping for good pictures

They crowd close and applaud
The lava as it rolls through groves
Of fruit and walnut trees and homes.

From Thucydides:

About the same time in the spring,
Before the grain was fully ripe
The Peloponnesians

Commanded by the Spartan king
Invaded Attica again
Settled down and laid waste the land.

And from the letters of old friends
Certain themes emerge, certain human traits:

She's so pretty but she can hardly hear
And she'll fall if she tries to dance.
Something to do with her inner ear.

The German doctors had her
When she was a child during the war
And wouldn't let her urinate.

The Unicorn

I. The Unicorn in Darkest Africa

'Fords are always picturesque,'

R. F. Burton wrote in 1858,
describing his crossing
of the Rusugi River.

'We crossed as usual
on a *unicorn* of negroids,

the upper part of the body
supported by two men,

and the feet resting upon
the shoulders of a third —

a posture somewhat similar
to that affected
by gentlemen who find themselves
unable to pull off their own boots.'

II. The Unicorn in Captivity

'Yesterday I saw this old black woman
on 96th and Broadway,'

my friend writes.

'She was out of her skull,
cursing and screaming
and stretching out her neck to spit.

And she was *white*! I mean
she had on a white shirt,
white shorts, white shoes, white socks,
a white rag around her head

and white shoe polish
on her face, her throat,
her hands, her legs,
any part of her skin that showed.'

Plea

To my friend
who can no longer see
animals in the clouds

and takes it
as a sign of madness:

Hang on. Keep watch.

They must be gathering now
over the Pacific,

great, soft herds of elephants,
cirrous alligators
and horses being pulled apart

with no pain.

To My Rival

I dreamed we were sitting
Waist-high in hot water,
Hotter than we could stand.

It was steaming.
You were at one end of a long tin tub,
I at the other. And we had to pull a rope

Back and forth between us. A thick rope.
Thicker than his penis.
Then we were in bed together,

Just you and I,
In warm, dry flannel nighties.
Curled up back to back. Asleep.

Linen, Bread and Wine

I've fallen in love again,
this time with German,
Stifter's *Erzählungen* to be exact.

In one of them, *Das Heidedorf*,
a boy leaves home

for the same reasons we all leave home
after years of leaning on the doorpost

half in, half out, fierce, vague . . .

'His mind longed for the taste of its bread, knowledge,
and his heart for the taste of love, its wine.'

Brote und Weine: with two words
he transforms rebellion into sacrament.

In another story he devotes pages
to the linen of a great, proud house,

describing the washing,
the spreading on bushes,

the mending, the folding, the counting,
the scenting, the stacking in great chests

of the scores of dazzling sheets
by the mistress, her two daughters and the maids.

Then, in detail, the slow decline,
the selling of the linens piece by piece

to strangers, who would casually display
the red-gold stitching of the crest.

Toward the End

Toward the end
her poems come closer
and closer together,

one every four minutes,
one every three.

She tries to control them
by breathing deeply
after each one,

by taking stock,
as they have told her to,
of her immense accomplishment.

She knows she should smile at her husband
for being brave enough
to come with her this far.

But she is beyond him now.
Alone, pulled by her monster baby death,
she becomes a slick red sheath,

a cone of pure pain.

III

Flight

One day you were there, the next day gone,
like that diamond I lost in the garbage.

A comet swinging wide, picking up speed,
you flashed across my planet path
while I was still plotting defenses:

what to conceal, what to reveal, taking my time
just when every second hurt you more.

Skinned by that pure self-loathing that fell on you
like knives, you moved among us, aping our ease.

How long had you been faking it? Now,
I make each gesture, every word a clue.

That Summer

That summer
after you hanged yourself
without asking
anyone who loved you
if they could bear it

I found myself dragging hoses
watering every inch
of this huge lawn
over and over
day after perfect day

obsessed
unable to let one more thing
one single blade of grass
die.

*'Where is there a sea left in which I can
really drown. I mean a person.'*
                              —Nietzsche

You came on strong straight up the shore,
holding high tide in your high-strung hands,
praising, setting up a tiny mirror
on the tip of each wave.

Swamped, I didn't see you slide away,
back to your deep, desperate work:
keeping your monsters covered with tons
of sheer and shifting will.

No use. One day they surfaced, burst and slopped
and you dragged yourself, a Sargasso
of shimmering guts, to that shed to drift
by the neck until dead.

They said self-inflicted, but I . . .
But some nights when all my drugs, even Mozart, fail
I crawl down to you and dive and dive
until my lungs fill and I drown.

First Autumn

The girl who fed
The swans last winter is dead
And they're gliding toward me,
Dragging cold, gray Vs
Across the stiffening cove.

The cob advances,
Rears, presents his dazzling chest
And I see how it was:
No rustle of silks,
Moist lips parted in ecstasy;

Her suicide surprised her
From behind, pinned the back
Of her neck in his beak
And forced her face down
In the shuddering mud.

Winter Games

I can skate on my life for days,
all torso and strong, straight leg
flung rigid at the sky.

Clear-eyed Athena in snug-fitting skin,
I cut the compulsory figures,
then glide into the grand finale,
that twirl executed at such high speed
I'm a tingling top.

Thighs sprout from my chest
and my head's a spinning globe of flesh
facing out, out, all ways at once.

Bravo! Bravissimo!
Quasimodo caught in a short, cute cape,
suddenly stone deaf, I sag away
to squat beside the breathing hole
of the sleek, sad beast that knows my name.

Anniversary

Already, in just a year,
your suicide has become
something that happened to me.

That's progress, I suppose.

I even have,
somewhere in the back of my mind,
the capstone consolation image
for the last poem
I'm going to write about you.

It's half mine, half Fellini:
an express train from Milan
arrives in parched Naples
with snow in all its crevices
and the people surround it,
press handfuls to their mouths,
their cheeks, their throats, and are refreshed.

But it's not working out.

When I think of it now,
giving you my poems to read
so you could see clear through me to my soul,
that magnificent, swift animal
pounding down the track
against terrific odds — to win!

See, here's a photo of my finish.

So in My Dream

You killed yourself
so in my dream

I introduced your husband
to a new, exciting woman

who was you.

IV

Gynecologist

Silently,
as pure
as this rough linen tent
we share

you lean into me,
your work.

Your eyes shift,
then go blind
as you become
all touch

and exquisitely
detached

a Flemish angel
suspended in the light
above me
on mighty, multicolored wings.

The Carpenters

The sensation of the tip of the cervix of the im-
pregnated uterus to the touch is like that of touch-
ing the lips. Feels soft like velvet, but deeper, beyond the softness, is a hardness as of board.
— *Taber's Cyclopedic Medical Dictionary*

Doctor number one takes his time,
makes himself at home.

His ceiling is large-curd cottage cheese,
my breasts are chandeliers
and he really digs
swinging on them,
telling me what I know already:

that they're swollen and they hurt
and how could he abort me?
He has ten lovely kids of his own.

Doctor number two makes sure
I'm sufficiently grateful,
then deftly delivers me of my check.

He decides we'll be tough together.
He shows me a cross-section
of a 'gal's uterus,'
tells me he could zap my tubes
for fifty dollars more

and we get down to the business
of ordering an O. R.
and softening the endometrium
by inserting a Japanese rod
of seaweed and bamboo.

I hold very still,
sweating out every inch
of this little haiku.

Now he's using rubber-coated fingers.
Now he's using steel.

Now two witnesses
are phoning 'the man responsible'
and he's giving them permission
to go ahead and work on me.

He's dazed, I think.
Like the rest of these Johns
he can believe in the softness
but not in the hardness just beyond.

Now I'm ready for repairs.
Strapped in stirrups
designed for some Amazon
I slide into a depression
that tips my cunt toward him
at precisely the angle he wants.

Four long needles later
I'm numb enough.

'Now I'm lifting up the uterus
with tongs,' he says. Okay.
'That washboard sensation is the scraping . . .'

Okay, I'm a melon rind
and he's a greedy boy
going after every speck. Okay.

I'm with him right up to the suction,
when he inserts a vacuum tube
and the walls of that jar are suddenly
bright red with gobs of high-speed gore.

I awake in the fetal position,
suspicious of everyone.

My thighs embrace like sisters
reunited after a long war.
They promise never to part.

'You'll bleed for a week,'
the foreman says as he leaves the job.
'Nothing up there for four weeks after that
And I'll see you back here in six.'

I'll be here.
I need these union carpenters, these men,
each with his own set of tools
for taking care of me
when I need a fix.

Out of Sync

And on the tenth day
the fertilized egg took control
of the glands, the blood,
all functions but the brain,

which hired an assassin
to tie down my legs,
those careless sentries,
and kill the prince.

He's dead,
but the blue and white queens,
my programmed breasts,
don't know it for a week

and go on singing,
swelling, expecting him,
preparing him a milk nest
cell by cell.

D & C

1

The O. R. clock still shows 1:28.
But this time its face is broken
And a magnified thumb,
Meaty pink ridges, smooth red troughs,
Is impaled on the minute hand,
Trembling, straining to hold it back.

2

A boy on the Lower East Side
Is shooting buckets
Against a grubby, red-brick wall.
The ball arcs high, misses the rim,
Becomes soft, becomes the boy,
Who has to fall now, all that way.

The Office

There were lots of women in the waiting room.
I had to wait a long time and I got bored.

Then it was my turn to climb up on the table
And for once they let me keep my pants on.

The child I refused to have was in my arms.
This time it was a girl. They were watching me

So I stroked and caressed the delicate skull
While the doctor felt gently for lumps in my breast.

'I notice you breathe easily,' he said.
'I'm old now and have to fight for every breath.'

If I had to do that, I said to myself
In my dream, I would rather be dead. Then I was.

V

I'm Trying

I'm trying to write
A letter to you

To you who gave me so much pain
It pooled and spilled over,
Scalding everyone around me

But I can't do it

In my dream
You kissed me on the mouth

I'm sitting here,
Helpless hatred
Leaking from my every pore
Like poison,
Like a deadly gas escaping

Building

Building

Bulging the walls

God, if only
You would walk up right now,
Open the door

And blow us both
Clean off the earth

Letter

I'm trying to figure you out.
What did you want from me?

I excite you? Shit!
I've got gray hair and stretch marks for starters.

Want to hear more? I don't even know
what it is that women do together.

The night you propositioned me
I dreamt of bees

with hugh, black, fuzzy testicles
that dragged them down

onto a mossy, sunlit shingled roof
then split open, then had lips from which

tiny bees, fully formed, began to slip.
Is that what you want, control of my dreams?

I was numb for a week
if it makes you happy,

my nerve endings a field of wheat
trampled by a twitching, smooth-assed horse.

You rode back to your castle on the hill,
laughing at your sheer audacity—

'That's the first time I made my move
with the husband right there in the room!'

I'm still staring after you,
a ruined peasant too stunned to raise my fist.

The Cane Mill

I was a zombie for weeks
After that hit and run

Reporting for work
In the cane mill each day

And pressing my chest
Against the thick spokes

Of the wheel made me numb

At night I lay down
In the dirt of my grave

And went over and over
What you had done

Until I got it right
Until it came to me

That the trickle of sugar
Belongs to the masters

And you are a master
An immaculate monster

Your whole body's a lash
And you use it, not dreaming

How much it can hurt

I Used To Have Fur

I used to have fur
and dimensions
and handles

I got drunk at parties
and let people in

Now I know better

Now I'm a sphere
made of plates
of vanadium poems

I'm almost completed

Don't worry
someone inside me
has memorized your gestures, your face

But see how your hands
glance off me now

and how your words are filed
and worked on
and bolted into place

The War of the Insects

The war of the insects
started at night,
inside my chest.

A butterfly killed and ate
something small and fluttery.

Then it emerged and began to grapple
with a creature like a dragonfly

but more compact.

Its wings were cobalt tapestry,
its six hinged legs sleek black.

Tough as a tank
it tucked itself in
then leaped,

landed on the butterfly's back
and started to drill a hole in its head.

A jet of scalding steam shot up.

The butterfly,
in agony,
tried everything:

became huge as a magpie,
black and white, magnificently plumed

and threw itself
against the walls,
the chairs of my room —
to no avail. The blue one clung
and drilled and drilled and drilled.

It was you and I as Yellowstone, of course
— the steam, those blues —

and also locked
in mortal combat

and I lose.